HELLO MY LITTLE POPPY SEED

An Expectant Mother's Love Poem

Dedicated to my children, Amy and Joshua,
and to my granddaughters, Madison and Mia

Copyright © 2020 by SwanCygnet Unlimited

Layout and Graphics by Amy E. Malczewski

All rights reserved. No portion of this book may be reproduced, transmitted, or stored in an information retrieval system in any form or by any means, graphic, electronic, or mechanical, including photocopying, taping, and recording, without prior written permission from the publisher.

ISBN 978-0-578-67789-7

Noodle Nana

a division of
www.swancygnet.com

Hello my little poppy seed.
I don't even know you're there.

Nest softly deep inside me
and trust that I will care
enough to keep you safe from harm
while you my body share.

Hello my little apple seed.

**Today your heart began
to beat its steady rhythm
and I began to plan
our future life together
so we have all the fun we can.**

Hello my little blueberry.
Your arms and legs now form.

You're becoming quite a person
while my body keeps you warm.

Will you be shy and serious,
or transfix us with your charm?

Hello my little raspberry.
This week your fingers sprout.

I wonder if you feel how much
my love for you pours out.

I love you more than life itself,
of that I have no doubt.

Hello my little strawberry.
Are you a girl or boy?

It really does not matter since
you fill my heart with joy.

I wonder how your laugh will sound
when you hold your favorite toy.

Hello my little kumquat.

Even though you are still quite small,
your tiny lungs begin to work,
and each day you surprise us all.

As you practice your first breaths,
our hearts you do enthrall.

Hello my little nectarine.
What does the future hold for you?

Only time will tell us.
I wait each day for some new clue.

Will your hair be golden?
Will your eyes be green or blue?

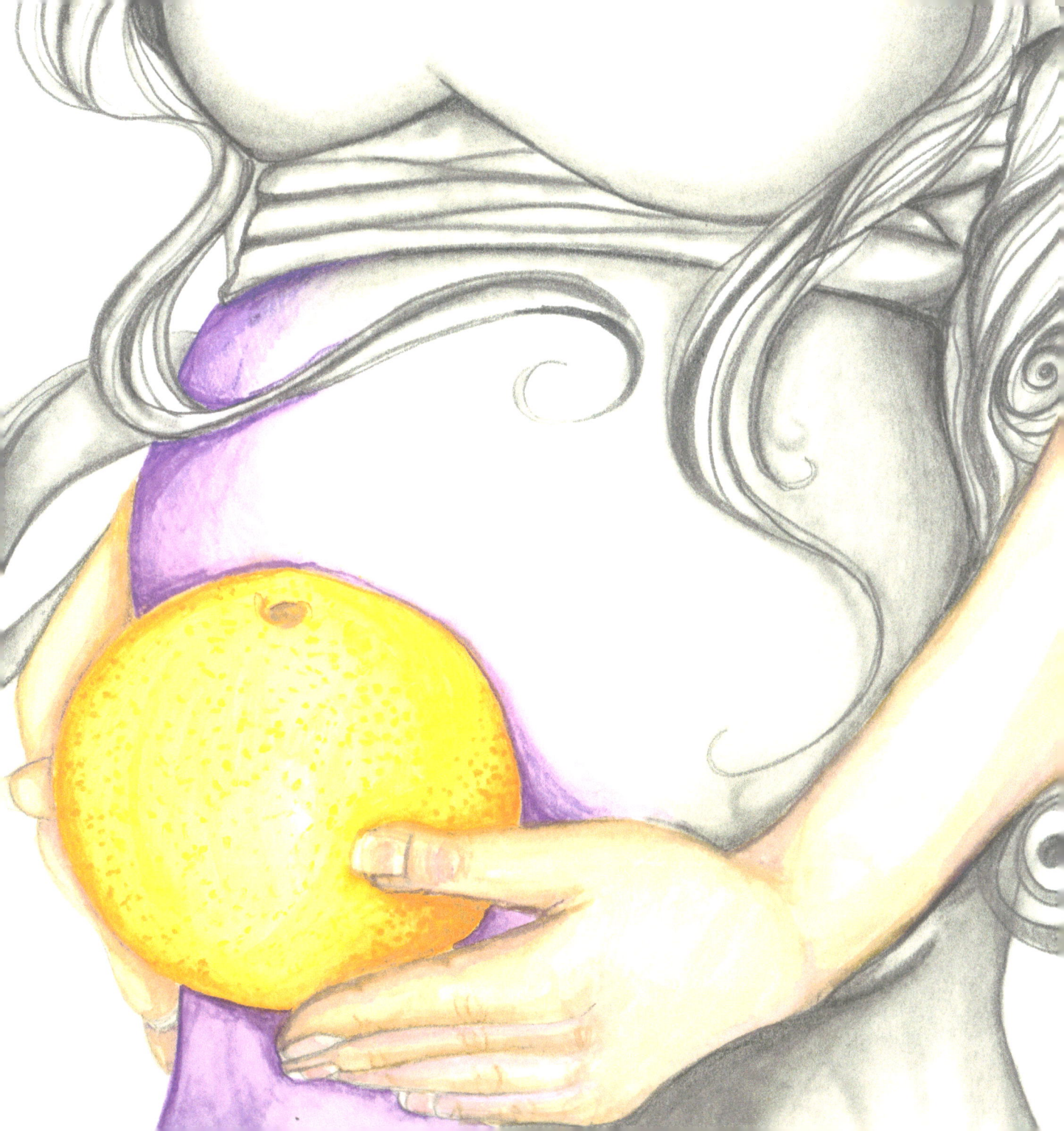

Hello my little cantaloupe.
Are those hiccups that I feel?

My excitement keeps on growing
with each movement you reveal.

My love is always steadfast.
It is constant. It is real.

Hello my little watermelon.
You are only days away.

I'll soon count your tiny fingers
and hold you as I sway
you gently in my loving arms
and bless your birthing day.

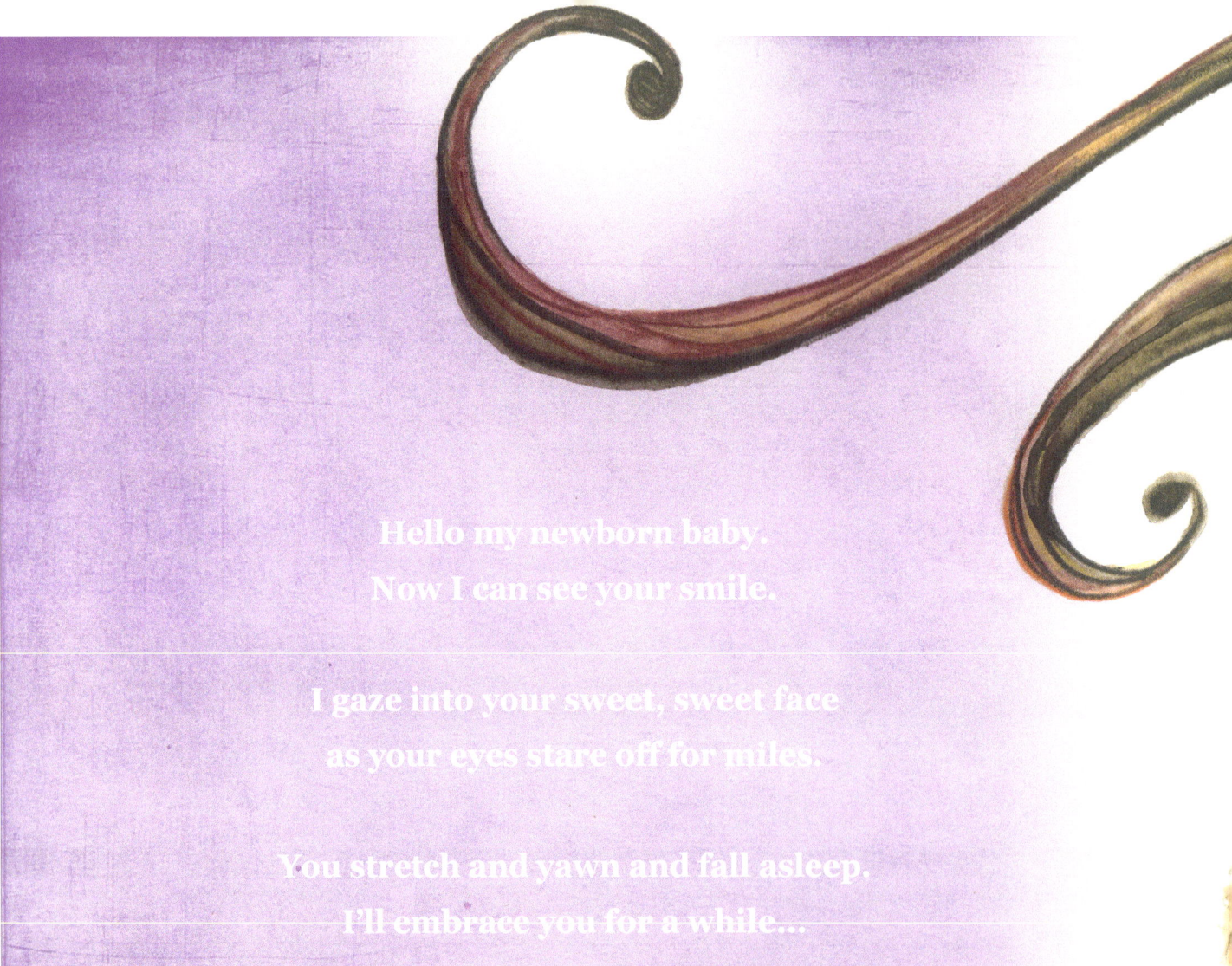

Hello my newborn baby.
Now I can see your smile.

I gaze into your sweet, sweet face
as your eyes stare off for miles.

You stretch and yawn and fall asleep.
I'll embrace you for a while...

baby's name

due date
birth date